A 30 MIN
ANALYSIS OF THE KEY CONCEPTS
IN

Medical Medium: Secrets Behind Chronic and Mystery Illness and How to Finally Heal by Anthony William

By High Speed Reads

Table of Contents

Introduction

ABOUT THE BOOK AND AUTHOR

The author, Anthony William, is a lay person chosen by "The Spirit of the Most High" to help human kind by identifying causes for their illnesses and how to cure them. Anthony stresses that he knows nothing about medicine, the human body or illnesses other than what Spirit – the name by which he calls "The Spirit of the Most High" - tells him. He also claims that Spirit is 100 percent accurate as he is second only to God himself.

The secrets revealed in this book are meant to fast-forward medical science research and help people live healthier and longer lives. The author describes his journey with the Spirit, which started when he was 4 years old and reveals secrets about illnesses that have remained until now unknown and incurable.

By revealing their true causes, he discloses that all these diseases that previously were symptomatically addressed are now curable, giving millions of people the opportunity to live better and longer lives.

OVERALL SUMMARY

There are four major parts to this book. Each part takes you deeper into the secrets that cause illnesses and explains the causes in great detail. You will find nowhere in this book advice that is anti-science or medicine. Rather, it explains illnesses in scientific terms, while pointing out the things that

1

science of today has overlooked – and hence, allowing for certain illnesses to plague the human body for decades.

Part I explains the origin of this book. It starts with details about the author, Anthony William, and how he gained the knowledge about healing the human body. It explains his connection to The Spirit of the Most High and how he is guided and taught to scan the human body to find the mystery illnesses within.

Part II introduces you to the actual reason behind a number of "mystery illnesses", i.e. the Epstein-Barr virus or the EBV. The author states with full authority and conviction that it is the EBV that is at the root of many devastating diseases that have plagued mankind, especially women, for so long. Among the diseases he names are multiple sclerosis, chronic fatigue syndrome, fibromyalgia, rheumatoid arthritis and thyroid problems. Anthony identifies the EBV as the mystery behind all mystery illnesses; all of the above diseases being symptoms of viral infections or different strains of the EBV.

Part III takes you through more diseases that are caused by EBV such as Type 2 diabetes, adrenal fatigue, candida, migraines, shingles, ADHD and autism, PTSD, depression, PSM and Lyme disease.

Every disease Anthony mentions has at the end suggestions of "healthy and healing foods" that the author recommends for healing. He assures that these illnesses have been and can be completely cured with the help of natural means, mostly change of diet, lifestyle and understanding about what exactly is the cause of their troubles.

Part IV tells about solutions. It talks about how you can prevent, recover and evolve into the "real you" in all possible ways, but mostly it focuses on how you can get better – physically and spiritually. Here you will learn how to ensure good health. It teaches how to cleanse, detoxify, discover hidden ingredients that would cause you harm and prevent healing, identify and use the most powerful foods and so on.

This part also teaches how to heal your soul without being religious. It brings to you methods on how to connect to angels, ask and get their help. It also gives simple and easy-to-follow instructions about meditation and other spiritual techniques that bring peace to the mind and soul.

You will find throughout the book a sprinkle of case studies that are heart-warming and inspiring. Each case study brings to light two major facts – one, that you are not alone suffering from diseases that have been misdiagnosed and continue to hurt you in spite of medical treatment and disciplined living; and two, that each one of these "mystery diseases" can be completely cured by natural and simple means.

Part I

There are two chapters in Part I, Chapter 1, which talks about how the author, Anthony Williams receives his powers, and Chapter 2, which talks about the truth behind mystery illnesses – illnesses, which are either unexplained or perennially misdiagnosed by the present-day medical science.

CHAPTER 1: ORIGINS OF THE MEDICAL MEDIUM

Summary

It all started when Anthony was 4 years old, he suddenly heard the voice of an old man, which seemed to be just outside his ear. The voice was never inside his mind; it was real and it was always from outside.

This person introduced himself as the "Spirit of the Most High"

The Spirit told him – at the age of four – to touch his grandmother's chest and say, "lung cancer". This was the only time Anthony saw Spirit – the name he calls his Spiritual Guide. He describes the Spirit as an old man with grey hair and a beard wearing an old brown robe. Needless to say, his grandmother, after undergoing the necessary tests, finds out that indeed she is suffering from lung cancer.

The Spirit continues to speak with Anthony as he grows up. He proceeds to teach him how to "see" diseases and what cures them. When asked who he was, Sprit tells Anthony that he is a word, Compassion. He said that he was the essence of the word, "Compassion" and as such second to only God, who is Love. While explaining that every word has energy and can be personified, Spirit tells Anthony that there are others like him such as, Faith, Joy, Hope, Peace, and more.

Anthony resented that he had been singled out by Spirit for this gift. He resented that he was robbed of his childhood, he resented that he had no privacy, he resented that he could see illnesses in every person around him like his parents, friends and even his girlfriend.

One day Anthony decides to go over Spirits head. He tries to appeal to God to remove Spirit from his life, his prayers go unanswered. Besides reading bodies to identify diseases, Anthony learns how to repair cars. Even that becomes a source of stress as in time he realizes that people are willing to invest more both emotionally and financially in their cars than in their own health.

There was a specific point in Anthony's life when he accepted his fate and commits to Spirit to be a Medical Medium in return for the life of his dog, whom Spirit saves from certain death. From that day onward he is fully dedicated to his gift, not only checking for physical health but also scanning the soul and heart to ensure complete healing.

Recap of Chapter 1

1. The author gains his special powers from "The Spirit of the Most High", a being who claims to be next to only God.

2. The Spirit, constantly talks to Anthony telling him clearly and accurately what the diagnosis is, what causes it and how it can be cured.

3. The Spirit also helped Anthony repair cars.

4. Anthony Williams commits to his gift and agrees to be the Medical Medium, as Spirit wants, in exchange for the life of his dog, Augustine whom Spirit saves.

CHAPTER 2: THE TRUTH ABOUT MYSTERY ILLNESSES

Summary

Though there are many diseases that do not yet have viable names, cures or hope by the standard of today's science, it is possible to find relief with the help of Spirit.

Any disease that has no cure or appropriate treatment (that alleviates its symptoms) is labeled as "mystery illness". Under this label are grouped diseases that have common names but no real cure such as, leaky gut syndrome, shingles, Bell's palsy, PTSD, ADHD, menopause complications, Candida, hypoglycemia, and Type2 diabetes among others.

The human body has been created to repair itself. Hence, all references to autoimmune diseases are wrong. The body never attacks itself. When it seems to do so, it is a clear indication that the enemy (factors that cause infection) is hiding in the area where the body seems to be attacking and medical science is incapable to identify it – yet.

Mystery illnesses are of three types – unnamed diseases, diseases that have ineffective treatment and misdiagnosed diseases.

The unnamed diseases are those which baffle doctors and have them say, "It's all in your head." This frustrates the patient because the symptoms are real, the pains are real, the discomforts are real – yet, he/she cannot prove it medically and neither can he/she hope for a cure.

The diseases that come with ineffective treatment are those that are recognized by the medical fraternity but have no definite cure. Often, instead of ameliorating the symptoms, the treatment actually worsens them. At the very best, the symptoms are managed, but the disease does not get any better.

When it comes to the misdiagnosed diseases, the patient will receive the name of a disease and a known treatment. However, since the disease is not diagnosed correctly in the first place, there is no hope of cure. If you are lucky you'll get relief for some of the symptoms, but they usually return or worsen over time.

Spirit knows the answer every time and he wants humanity to learn the reason behind all these baffling diseases that seem to confuse doctors.

Recap of Chapter 2:

1. Millions of people worldwide suffer from mystery diseases.

2. There are three types of mystery illnesses, i.e. diseases that have no name (yet), diseases which have no effective treatment, and diseases that are misdiagnosed.

3. It is NOT true that the body attacks itself. All diseases that fall under the category of autoimmune diseases are mystery illnesses.

4. It is NOT in your head; the symptoms you feel are true, even when doctors have no valid answers.

5. Spirit has all the answers and he wants the world to benefit from this knowledge through Anthony Williams.

6. You can be healed of whatever diseases you are suffering from.

PART II

Part II has four chapters, each one addressing a particular difficult or baffling disease, i.e. Epstein-Barr Virus, Chronic Fatigue Syndrome, Fibromyalgia, Multiple Sclerosis, Rheumatoid Arthritis (RA), Hypothyroidism and Hashimoto's Thyroiditis.

CHAPTER 3: EPSTEIN BARR VIRUS, CHRONIC FATIGUE SYNDROME AND FIBROMYALGIA

In this chapter you learn about the main culprit behind mystery illnesses – the Epstein-Barr Virus or EBV as it is popularly known. You learn all about its origin, types, stages and that it is completely curable.

Summary

The mystery behind the mystery illnesses is ONE VIRUS, known as the Epstein-Barr Virus or EBV. Unknown to medical science of today, the EBV goes through four stages.

In stage one the virus replicates itself and readies itself to attack. The virus is most vulnerable in this stage, but unfortunately because it causes almost no symptoms it cannot be caught at this time.

Stage two has the EBV turn into mononucleosis, which is also called the "kissing disease". Unfortunately, today's medical science is not aware that this is stage two of EBV. Another thing which the doctors do not know is that EBV has a "friend" who works along with it while attacking the body, i.e. the bacteria strain called Streptococcus. Hence, your body ends up fighting two separate entities – virus and bacteria, which both confuses and strains the in. system. In this stage, the virus will seek to hide in a n. organ such as the liver or spleen – because it has easy acc⌐₀s to toxins there and toxins are its major source of strength.

Stage three has the virus settling happily in the organ of its choice, making it completely invisible to the tests known today. It is assumed at this stage that you are cured and there is nothing to worry about. As it nests there the EBV will be busy creating three types of toxins that will poison your body, i.e. its excretion, its dead cells and the production of neurotoxin. These toxins confuse the immune system and weaken it.

The virus waits for a trigger before launching a full attack, such as heartbreak, mental breakdown, pregnancy, menopause, childbirth, accident, death of a loved one, etc. Lupus and hypothyroidism are the symptoms of this attack. EBV thrives on adrenaline; hence it loves to stress the adrenal glands.

Stage four has the virus go for the central nervous system – which is its primary goal. Diseases such as Chronic Fatigue Syndrome, Fibromyalgia, Tinnitus, Vertigo and Meniere's disease – are all EBV virus at work. There are more than 60 strains of this virus, which can be grouped into six major groups.

Group 1 has the strain that is slowest. It takes decades for the virus to move through the four stages, and the symptoms may be not surface until you are in your 70s or 80s. In some cases, the EBV may remain in stage 2 and never get to 3 and 4.

Group 2 will show symptoms when you reach your 50s. This is the only strain of EBV that the medical fraternity knows of today.

Group 3 will act up as you cross your 40s and cause problems such as vertigo, joint pains, fatigue, heart palpitations, etc.

Group 4 comes with symptoms showing as early as your 30s. Besides all the symptoms of Groups 1-3, this type of EBV strain also causes chronic fatigue, anxiety, brain fog, fibromyalgia, moodiness, and confusion among others.

Groups 5 hits people in their 20s and is often the reason for doctors to say, "It's all in your head" because all seems fine, yet there are so many complaints about your health. As the patient experiences fear and worry, the virus grows stronger.

Group 6 is the worst of all and shows symptoms even in children and causes serious misdiagnosis such as lupus, viral meningitis, leukemia, etc.

The good news is that EBV can be destroyed and you can regain your complete health with the help of natural (and healing) foods. The time may vary from 3 months to 18 months, but the cure is complete. A list of the best healing foods and supplements is given below that can eliminate the virus and all its negative effects on your body.

Healing Foods (Eat at least 3 of these foods daily alternating your consumption)

-**Wild blueberries:** Restorative for the central nervous system. Flush neurotoxins out of liver.

-Celery: strengthens stomach acid and is a source of mineral salts to the central nervous system.

-Sprouts: Helps fight EBV by providing zinc and selenium to your immune system.

-Asparagus: Renews the liver and spleen; makes the pancreas stronger.

-Spinach: provides absorbable micronutrients to the nervous system.

-Cilantro: removes EBV's favorite foods mercury and lead.

-Parsley: removes aluminum & copper.

-Coconut oil: antiviral and anti-inflammatory to help fight EBV.

-Garlic: antibacterial & antiviral that fights EBV.

-Ginger: relieves spasms associated with EBV & helps assimilate nutrients.

-Raspberries: contains antioxidants that remove free radicals from the bloodstream & organs.

-Lettuce: cleans EBV from the liver and helps stimulate peristaltic action in the intestines.

-Papayas: restore stomach acids and the central nervous system.

-Apricots: rebuilds the immune system and strengthens the blood.

-Pomegranates: detoxes the lymphatic system and the blood

-Grapefruit: contains calcium & bioflavonoids that support the immune system.

-Kale: Contains specific alkaloids that protect against EBV and other viruses.

-Sweet potatoes: detoxes the liver from EBV byproducts.

-Cucumbers: Flushes neurotoxins from the bloodstream & strengthens the kidneys & adrenals.

-Fennel: Helps to fight off EBV with its strong antiviral compounds.

Healing herbs and Supplements (The following will strengthen your immune system & help you heal)

-Cat's claw: reduces EBV and cofactors.

-Silver hydrosol: have antiviral effects.

-Zinc: protects the thyroid & strengthens the immune system.

-Vitamin B12 (methylcobalamin and/ or adenosylcobalamin): boosts the central nervous system.

-Licorice root: strengthens kidneys and adrenals, lowers production of EBV.

-Lemon balm: strengthens the immune system & Kills EBV cells.

-5-MTHF (5-methyltetrahydrofolate): strengthen the central nervous system & endocrine system

- Selenium: strengthens the central nervous system.

-Red marine algae: strong antiviral that removes heavy metals

- L-lysine: serves as a anti-inflammatory for the central nervous system & lowers EBV load

-Spirulina (from Hawaii): eliminates heavy metals and helps rebuild central nervous system

-Ester-C: removes EBV toxins from the liver & boosts immune system.

-Nettle leaf: gives the brain, blood, and central nervous system vital micronutrients.

-Monolaurin: reduces EBV cofactors and breaks down load. Also antiviral

-Elderberry: boosts the immune system and antiviral

-Red clover: removes EBV neurotoxins from the liver, lymphatic system, and spleen

-Star anise: helps remove EBV from the thyroid and liver. Also antiviral

-Curcumin: helps boost the central nervous system & endocrine system.

Recap of Chapter 3:

1. Discovered in 1964, the EBV has been around since the 1900's and has mutated a lot since then.

2. The medical fraternity knows about only ONE strain of the EBV; there are more than 60 varieties, which are not yet discovered.

3. More than 225 million people in the USA alone suffer from some type of EBV.

4. The 60 varieties are grouped into 6 groups with roughly 10 types per group.

5. The ultimate goal of the EBV is to reach and inflame your central nervous system.

6. There are 4 stages of the EBV infection; it takes sometimes decades for the virus to move from one stage to another.

7. EBV is easily curable; the difficult part is to find it.

CHAPTER 4: MULTIPLE SCLEROSIS

Summary

MS is a disease that affects the message facilitator of the central nervous system, i.e. the myelin sheath. When this happens, the messages to the brain becomes scrambled causing pain, mental problems, paralysis, bowel dysfunction, vision problems and depression among others.

Correct diagnosis is important and MS if often a label wrongly given to other diseases. MS is in most cases a misdiagnosed attack of the EBV. To be sure it is EBV and not MS, look for the cofactors that are normally associated with the EBV, i.e. streptococcus, H.pylori, Candida, Cytomegalovirus and presence of heavy metals (mercury, copper and aluminum). If none of these are present, then it might actually be MS; but if these are identified, rest assured that you are suffering from EBV and you can be completely cured.

Healing is possible both for MS and for the misdiagnosed EBV. A list of healing supplements that will protect your myelin sheath and reduce pain while you heal from EBV is listed below. The cure can be achieved within 3-18 months.

Healing Supplements

-EPA & DHA (eicosapentaenoic acid and docosahexaenoic acid) :Buy the plant based version

-L-glutamine: Protects Neurons and removes toxins from the brain

-ALA (alpha lipoic acid) Helps repair the Myelin nerve sheath

-Monolaurin: Removes virus cells and bacteria cells from the brain

-Curcumin : Relieves pain and reduces inflammation of the nervous system

-Barley grass juice extract powder: Helps feed the Myelin nerve sheath and central nervous system

Recap of Chapter 4:

1. Multiple sclerosis is often EBV misdiagnosed.

2. MS (misdiagnosed or real) is completely curable; with the right foods and supplements, you can be free from it in 3-18 months depending upon your condition.

3. To confirm that your MS is actually EBV, you may look for signs of cofactors in the body such as streptococcus, H.pylori, Candida, Cytomegalovirus and presence of heavy metals (mercury, copper and aluminum).

CHAPTER 5: RHEUMATOID ARTHRITIS

Summary

Rheumatoid arthritis is defined by inflammation of joints. This is an affliction that affects about 2.5 million Americans in the age group of 15-60. Doctors wrongly assume that this is an autoimmune disease. It is not. It is important to keep in mind that the body never attacks itself. When it seems to do so, you need to look very closely and you will find that there are other pathogens that your body identified and wants to eliminate.

The tests used to identify RA are not adequate as they are geared to measure the level of inflammation rather than identifying the underlying reason for the symptom. This is why the treatment is also wrong. Doctors prescribe immunosuppressant medicine, which actually help the virus grow rather than die.

It is possible to be completely cured of RA and it is easy to do so, too. The only problem that will stand between you and complete relief is the diagnosis. RA is actually a type of EBV – and as such, completely curable.

Healing Herbs & Supplements: (Natural anti-Inflammatories that will not weaken your immune system and will promote healing)

-Curcumin: reduces inflammation pain.

-Nettle leaf: reduces EBV specific inflammation with alkaloids

-Turmeric: relieves inflammation and pain.

-N-acetyl cysteine: reduces pain and inflammation.

-MSM (methylsulfonylmethane): reduces joint pain & inflammation.

*For additional pain relief use a cold pack for 30 minutes followed by a hot back for 10 minutes

Recap of Chapter 5:

1. Rheumatoid Arthritis is not an autoimmune disease since the body never attacks itself.

2. RA is completely curable, though the medical fraternity declared it as incurable.

3. The methods used today for diagnosing RA are not adequate.

4. RA is a form EBV and can be completely eliminated within 2-24 months.

CHAPTER 6: HYPOTHYROIDISM AND HASHOMOTO'S THYROIDISM

Summary

Thyroid problems are afflictions of the modern era. These types of diseases were not there prior to the 19th century. Pollution, refined foods and stressful life style is what depleted the body of many must-have nutrients making people vulnerable to many diseases including this one.

Hypothyroidism is the condition where the thyroid gland produces inadequate amounts of hormones. Hashimoto's disease is when the body seems to turn on itself and attack the thyroid gland. The body never turns on itself; this should be sign enough that there is an enemy hiding inside of it.

More than 95 percent of thyroid problems are caused directly by EBV; the other 5 percent may be from radiation. Unfortunately, the tests known today are highly inadequate to pinpoint the problem. Most doctors will start treatment even if the tests do not come back positive. However, to fully recover, you need to know and acknowledge the fact that the problem is due to viral infection.

It is possible to completely eliminate the virus from the body with the help of natural foods and achange in lifestyle. The body can repair itself very fast if helped along a little. Unfortunately, the medication available today actually helps the EBV more than the thyroid gland or the body. The most beneficial foods for thyroid health are cranberries, Brazil nuts, coconut oil, garlic, hemp seeds, sprouts, Atlantic dulse and wild blueberries. A list of healing herbs and supplements is given below.

Healing Herbs & Supplements

-Zinc: strengthens the thyroid and kills EBV cells

-Spirulina (from Hawaii): provides the thyroid with critical micronutrients

-Bladderwrack: provides the thyroid with trace minerals and iodine

-Chromium: stabilizes your endocrine system.

-L-tyrosine: increases the production of thyroid hormones.

-Ashwagandha: helps stabilize the endocrine system; strengthens the thyroid and adrenal glands

-Licorice root: aids the adrenal glands & removes EBV cells in the thyroid

-Eleuthero/Siberian ginseng: helps stabilize the endocrine system; strengthens the adrenal glands

-Lemon balm: slows nodule growth & removes EBV cells in the thyroid

-Manganese: helps in the production of thyroid hormone T3

-Selenium: assists in the production of thyroid hormone T4

-Vitamin D3: helps boost the immune system

-B-complex: provides necessary vitamins for the endocrine system.

-Magnesium: used to stabilize thyroid hormone T3.

-EPA & DHA (eicosapentaenoic acid and docosahexaenoic acid): buy plant based not fish based

-Bacopa monnieri: helps thyroid hormone production

-Rubidium: provides stability for thyroid hormone production.

-Copper: kills EBV and helps the effectiveness of iodine.

Recap of Chapter 6:

1. Hypothyroidism and Hashimoto's disease both are caused by the EBV.

2. Tests known today are not adequate for diagnosing thyroid problems.

3. Thyroid conditions caused by EBV are completely and easily curable. You can definitely get better.

PART III

Part III covers 10 chapters, each one describing one major disease, i.e. Type 2 Diabetes and Hypoglycemia, Adrenal fatigue, Candida, Migraines, Shingles, ADHD and Autism, Post Traumatic Stress Disorder, Depression, Premenstrual Syndrome and Menopause and Lyme Disease.

CHAPTER 7: TYPE 2 DIABETES AND HYPOGLYCEMIA

Summary

Type 2 diabetes and hypoglycemia start with the adrenal glands malfunctioning. The malfunction ends up damaging the pancreas and liver to such extent that you could remain suffering from the disease for life.

The biggest mistake is to eliminate sugar from your diet and replace it with a diet of high animal fat disguised as protein-based foods. To regain your health you need to understand that the enemy is the refined sugar and animal fat that is recommended (mistakenly so) as animal protein. With a high fat diet and no sugar you add stress to the liver and pancreas. For healing, you need to focus on getting your fuel – sugar/ glucose – from natural sources such as fruits. Fruits are forbidden to diabetic patients, but the truth is that these foods are the best healers.

There are certain foods to avoid – processed foods, eggs, processed oils, milk, cheese, but not fruits and honey. Natural sugars are important sources for fuel for the body and hence, highly recommended. Beneficial foods if you have hypoglycemia or type 2 diabetes include asparagus, kale, raspberries, sprouts, papayas, spinach, celery and blueberries.

Listed below are a number of healing herbs and supplements that are designed to help heal the body and eliminate these two diseases altogether.

Healing Herbs & Supplements

-**Zinc:** stabilizes glucose levels in the blood & supports the pancreas and adrenal glands.

-**Chromium:** stabilizes insulin levels & helps the pancreas and adrenal glands

-**Spirulina** (from Hawaii): helps the adrenal glands & supports glucose levels in the blood.

-**Ester-C:** supports & soothes the adrenal glands.

-**ALA** (alpha lipoic acid): supports the liver in storing and releasing glucose.

-**Silica:** assists the pancreas in the release of insulin.

-**Purslane:** helps the pancreas in its production of digestive enzymes.

-**Eleuthero** (aka Siberian ginseng): helps prevent the adrenal glands from overreacting to intense emotions.

-**Panax ginseng:** helps prevent the adrenal glands from overreacting to intense emotions.

-**EPA & DHA** (eicosapentaenoic acid and docosahexaenoic acid): Be sure to buy plant-based not fish based. Fights insulin resistance.

-Biotin: assists the central nervous system & helps stabilize glucose levels in the blood

-B-complex: supports your central nervous system.

-Gymnema sylvestre: helps stabilize insulin levels & lower glucose levels in the blood

-Magnesium: calms stressed adrenal glands & helps digestive problems caused by an underperforming pancreas.

-Vitamin D3: reduces inflammation and supports the pancreas and adrenal glands

Recap of Chapter 7:

1. Type 2 diabetes and hypoglycemia are not caused by sugar abuse. The problem starts with malfunctioning adrenal glands.

2. Besides a long list of healing foods, you should include fruits in your diet; it is the high-protein diet that causes you the most harm while the fruits heal.

3. Caught in time, both the pancreas and liver will regenerate as all damage is reversible.

4. Type 2 diabetes and hypoglycemia are totally curable.

CHAPTER 8: ADRENAL FATIGUE

Summary

Adrenal fatigue is when the adrenal glands are incapable of producing enough adrenaline, as required by the body. Stress is the topmost cause for this problem and that's not surprising with the life style of people today. Emotion is another factor that strains the adrenal glands and it is as bad, if not worse than stress. In some cases, this is the result of EBV infection.

The symptoms are varied. Feeling exhausted and wanting to sleep several times during the day while paradoxically, at night you have trouble sleeping. If you do sleep, you often still feel unrested in the morning. Feeling thirsty constantly and even sweating profusely are also symptoms.

The best way to restore the functioning of your adrenal glands is to remove yourself from stress. If you have undergone any strong emotional upheaval, soul healing meditation is recommended.

Healing is possible with a proper diet containing the right balance of sugar, potassium, sodium and the grazing style of eating. The "Grazing" method is when you replace the three meals of the day with smallish meals that you consume every 90-120 minutes. It is not recommended to cut out carbs – as presently advised by doctors.

Recovery can be expected in 2-24 months depending on your condition when you begin. The best foods to eat for adrenal fatigue are red skinned apples, romaine lettuce, raspberries, blackberries, broccoli, kale, bananas, wild blueberries, asparagus and sprouts. Listed below are herbs and supplements that will help in your recovery.

Healing Herbs & Supplements

-Licorice root: balances cortisone & cortisol

-Spirulina (from Hawaii): reinforces & strengthens the adrenals

-Ester-C: calms adrenal glands that have become enlarged and lowers inflammation.

-Chromium: strengthens the adrenal glands, pancreas and thyroid glands

-Eleuthero (aka Siberian ginseng): protects the adrenal glands from overreacting to stress by enhances the body's ability to react and adapt

-Schisandra: reduces adrenal gland stress by suppressing kidney spasms

-Ashwagandha: balances cortisol, testosterone and DHEA

-Magnesium: reduces adrenal gland stress by lowering anxiety

-5-MTHF (5-methyltetrahydrofolate): lightens strain on the adrenal glands

-Cordyceps: helps to strengthen the gallbladder and liver so they can effectively process excess cortisol in the bloodstream.

-Panax ginseng: helps protect the adrenal glands from overreacting to stress by increasing the body's ability to react and adapt

-Rose hips: Soothes adrenal glands that are enlarged from overexertion by lowering inflammation

-Barley grass juice extract powder: helps the adrenal glands by boosting the hydrochloric acid in the stomach

-Astragalus: strengthens both the endocrine & immune system

-Lemon balm: regulates the production of insulin and replenishes the nervous system

-Rhodiola: strengthens adrenal functions.

Recap of Chapter 8:

1. Adrenal fatigue is similar to mental breakdown (of the glands) and results in erratic production of adrenaline; it could be either too much or too less.

2. It is very important to address the mental and emotional condition while attempting to heal. Strong emotions (negative) are as bad as stress for the adrenal glands.

3. Complete healing is possible with natural foods and substances.

4. Meditation is recommended to enhance the ability of body and mind to handle stress and emotional upheavals.

5. In many instances, the underlying cause is an infection of the EBV, yet unknown to the medical fraternity.

CHAPTER 9: CANDIDA

Summary

Candida fungus was identified as the reason for a host of mystery symptoms as late as the early 90s. Every person has Candida, yeast which resides in the intestine whose main job is to help digestion and absorption of food. Like the sugar in the blood for Type 2 diabetes, Candida is the messenger. It is a cofactor to a number of major diseases such as Lyme disease, H.pylori, herpes, EBV, shingles, HHV-6, MS and so on.

Candida is used as a scapegoat for many diseases where doctors do not have an answer. While Candida can be found outside the gut, which is its home, it always means that there is some serious infection brewing somewhere in the body. Doctors advise against sugar for lack of better knowledge; however, not all sugar should be avoided. Sugar from fruits actually kills Candida. The ones that feed it are processed sugar, agave nectar, beet sugar, etc.

The advice to get on high-protein and high-fat diets is wrong as it actually feeds Candida. It is the opposite that will help control it, i.e. low fat, low protein and an abundance of fruit. You need to avoid antibiotics and anti-fungal medication as these will deplete your gut of the good bacteria and cause the opposite effect and cause a serious imbalance in your immune system.

To heal, you need to focus on rebuilding the gut flora, increase the levels of hydrochloric acid in your digestive fluids and detoxify your liver. If the reason for your Candida is the EBV, then healing is only a matter of time with the right foods and diet.

Recap of Chapter 9:

1. Everybody has Candida in their gut; it is a friendly and useful fungus, which lives in the gut and helps digestion.

2. When Candida comes positive in tests, it is always an indication of an underlying problem; this is a cofactor to many infections.

3. It is possible to get rid of Candida, but to do so you need to eat plenty of fruits and maintain a low fat, low protein diet.

4. No antibiotics or anti-fungal medication should be taken for Candida as this would produce the opposite effect.

CHAPTER 10: MIGRAINES

Summary

Migraines are the result of a cluster of 2-3 causes which come from stress, eating the wrong foods and heavy metals poisoning.

Besides the known triggers such as concussion, meningitis, stroke, TIA, brain aneurysm, brain tumor, impeded cervical nerves, there are many other major factors that cause migraines. These factors are not yet known to the medical fraternity as causes for migraines. You would have to navigate carefully through all your symptoms to identify the right trigger and then follow the method to cure it.

The triggers are many – EBV and Shingles, Micro-Transient Ischemic Attack, Sinus, Ammonia permeability, electrolyte deficiency, stress, menstrual cycle, sleep disorders, toxicity (heavy metals and others), migraine-happy foods and allergies. Food triggers for migraines are Chocolate, Alcohol, salt, oils, additives, fermented foods, gluten, eggs and dairy products.

Healing foods that prevent migraines are apples, cinnamon, ginger, kale, garlic, chili peppers, hemp seeds, papayas, cilantro and fresh celery juice. Listed below are herbs and supplements that will help you.

Healing Herbs & Supplements

-Chrysanthemum tea: reduces histamine by calming allergy based reactions

-Feverfew: keeps blood vessels balanced during migraine attacks

-**Butterbur:** strengthens the basophiles during migraines

-**Magnesium:** eases tension around the trigeminal nerves

-**Ester-C:** provides more oxygen to needed areas by removing histamines from the bloodstream

-**Ginkgo biloba**: reduces histamine by calming allergy based reactions

-**White willow bark:** reduces pain and inflammation

-**Kava-kava:** calms tense nerves.

-**Lemon balm:** Calms the central nervous system & lowers inflammation

-**Rosemary leaf:** provides blood vessel protection

-**Riboflavin** (Vitamin B2): helps nerve function.

-**Coenzyme Q10** (CoQ10): strengthens the nerves ability to send messages & lowers inflammation

-**Cayenne pepper:** maintain your histamine balance and relieves pain

-**Skullcap:** calms tense nerves.

-**Valerian root:** decreases hypertension associated with migraines; relaxes the vagus nerve

Recap of Chapter 10:

1. Migraines are often caused by a cluster of 2-3 factors; it is important to identify all triggers.

2. There are certain foods that aggravate/ trigger migraines; they need to be eliminated from the diet.

3. There are many other triggers - previously known by the medical fraternity – that cause migraines; careful investigation is required to identify the exact triggers.

4. It is possible to be completely cured of migraines with the right foods and supplements.

CHAPTER 11: SHINGLES – TRUE CAUSE OF COLITIS, TMJ, DIABETIC NEUROPATHY AND MORE

Summary

There are as many as 15 strains of shingles. They are divided into two major types, i.e. shingles with rashes and shingles without rashes. The shingles with rashes are named as per the location of appearance, i.e. you have classic shingles, upper body shingles, both arm shingles, one arm shingles, head shingles, both legs shingles and vaginal area shingles. These are the milder types of shingles, which the body can often fight on its own.

Among the varieties of shingles without rashes are - diabetic neuropathy or neuralgic shingles, maddening itch shingles, vaginal shingles, colitis shingles, arm and leg burning shingles, mouth shingles, TMJ and Bell's palsy, frozen shoulder shingles and body on fire shingles.

The healing method includes a number of herbs and foods such as wild blueberries, papayas, coconuts, avocados, green beans, lettuce, red skinned apples, pears, bananas, artichokes, sweet potatoes, asparagus and spinach. No antibiotics or any other medication that lowers the efficiency of the immune system should be taken. A list of healing herbs and supplements is below.

Healing Herbs & Supplements

-**ALA** (alpha lipoic acid): fortifies the nervous system

-**Magnesium:** soothes inflammation and nerves

-MSM (methylsulfonylmethane): restores nerve flexibility

-Vitamin B12 (as methylcobalamin and/ or adenosylcobalamin): strengthens the nervous system

-EPA & DHA (eicosapentaenoic acid and docosahexaenoic acid): strengthens the nervous system. Make sure you purchase plant based, not fish

-Lobelia: kills the virus immediately

-Feverfew: reduces nervous system inflammation

-California poppy: calms nerves

-Licorice root: slows the ability of virus cells to reproduce

-Zinc: reduces inflammatory responses to shingles neurotoxins

-L-lysine: slows the ability of virus cells to reproduce

-Selenium: repairs damaged nerves close to the skin

-Nettle leaf: soothes inflammation & pain caused by shingles rashes.

<u>Recap of Chapter 11:</u>

1. Shingles are often the underlying cause for many of the mystery illnesses of today, such as MS, colitis, Bell's palsy, Lyme disease and so on.

2. It is important that you avoid all medication that lowers the efficiency of your immune system.

3. It is possible to eliminate shingles from your system completely and permanently – with the food and supplements recommended.

CHAPTER 12: ATTENTION DEFICIT / HYPERACTIVITY DISORDER AND AUTISM

Summary

The two types of ADHD are inattentiveness and hyperactivity. While the former is more often associated with girls, the latter is more common in boys. It is also possible that one child has both types.

While modern medicine tends to put the blame on an unhealthy gut, the actual cause is heavy metal poisoning. When heavy metals, such as mercury and/ or aluminum settle in the midline that divided the two hemispheres of the brain, ADHD and autism occurs. These metals often are passed on from the parents as the toxins tend to remain in the body for generations passed on through genes.

The traditional treatment for ADHD and autism are amphetamines, which seemingly works fine. The reason for the success cannot be explained by the doctors yet. Amphetamines stimulate the adrenal glands to produce adrenaline, which is accepted by the brain as an equivalent for glucose. The brain of the child with ADHD and autism develops a huge number of adaptable neurons in the front lobe, which explains why the child is intuitive and at the same time tends to focus on self, more than others; too much information comes to the child and it exhausts him/her.

To heal avoid metal contamination, traditional sweets and all wheat products. You need to also avoid foods and additives such as aspartame, MSG, canola oil, corn, etc. that tend to be toxic to the body.

Healing foods include flax seeds, strawberries, avocados, blackberries, bananas, coconut oil, celery, wild blueberries and cilantro. A list of herbs and supplements is given below.

Healing Herbs & Supplements

-Spirulina (from Hawaii): removes heavy metals from the brain

-Vitamin B12 (methylcobalamin and/ or adenosylcobalamin): supports the central nervous system & brain

-Ester-C: helps repair damaged neurotransmitters and supports the adrenal glands.

-Zinc: supports neurotransmitters

-Melatonin: helps grow neurons and lowers inflammation in the brain

-Lemon balm: lowers inflammation, kills viruses & soothes the central nervous system

-Magnesium: assists in the ability to learn, remember, speak and think

-Ginkgo biloba: reduces inflammation in the brain and helps remove mercury

-GABA (gamma-Aminobutyric acid): enhances neurotransmitters and soothes the central nervous system

-B-complex: sustains the brain stem & brain

-Ginseng: strengthens the adrenal glands

-Probiotics: boosts the immune system

-EPA & DHA (eicosapentaenoic acid and docosahexaenoic acid): grows and repairs neurons. Purchase plant based version not fish based

Recap of Chapter 12:

1. The causes behind ADHD and autism are not well defined by the medical fraternity.

2. The ailments are the result of deposits of heavy metals in the canal that separates the right from the left brain hemispheres.

3. Healing foods, diet and detoxification is the path to healing for ADHD and autistic children.

CHAPTER 13: POST TRAUMATIC STRESS DISORDER

Summary

There are the two types of post-traumatic stress disorders (PTSD). The most common one is the one that you experience after serious danger – physical or emotional. The lesser known, but most common between the two is the unrecognized PTSD. This is the one that is not major, but unpleasant and hurtful nonetheless. It could be the hurt feeling that grows out of being rejected for the prom, or bad turbulence when a person is flying or even a case of food poisoning, etc.

These are not earth-shattering dangerous or emotional experiences, but they hurt and in most cases the feelings are buried inside. This causes the unrecognized PTSD; it is like a buried landmine that waits for the right trigger to explode. The feelings build on because they are not released affecting your vitality, immune system and brain function.

Though the medical community focuses on electrolyte imbalance as the primary cause, it is in fact, glucose deficiency that affects the brain in PTSD. There is a chemical imbalance and it is caused by glucose deficiency. Glucose is required to both prevent burn out from the overload of adrenaline in the brain and also to calm electrical storms triggered in the brain. Sugar has been used intuitively in PTSD – after breakups, during high-adrenaline sports, etc.

The problem is that with the surge comes the depletion and this is when depression sets in. Hence, while a boost of sugar can be an SOS approach, long term healing requires you to create new positive experiences to substitute for the bad ones. For help you could seek out the Angel of Restitution and/ or learn to meditate daily.

Foods that help heal PTSD include dates, raw honey, tangerines, apples, mangoes, figs, oranges, papayas, sweet potatoes, persimmons, bananas, melons, beets and wild blueberries. A list of herbal supplements is below.

Healing Herbs & Supplements

-**L-glutamine**: supports neural health and brain functions

-**5-MTHF** (5-methyltetrahydrofolate): helps the central nervous system

-**B-complex:** supports neurotransmitters & strengthens cognitive function

-**Ginkgo biloba:** strengthens neurotransmitters and neurons

-**GABA** (gamma-Aminobutyric acid): helps calm an overactive mind

-**Spirulina** (from Hawaii): restores brain tissue and helps repair the central nervous system

-**Honeysuckle:** balances glucose

-**Nettle leaf:** regulates an over-reactive endocrine system

-**Magnesium L-threonate:** strengthens cognitive functions

-**Siberian ginseng:** regulates & supports the endocrine system

Recap of Chapter 13:

1. There are two types of PTSD - the first type is that which the medical fraternity knows and treats and results from a major setback in the patient's life; the second type is the non-recognized PTSD or that the patient does not dwell on.

2. The main reason for the symptoms of PTSD is depletion of glucose – and not electrolytes as it is believed today.

3. Creating positive experiences as new reference points is one of the most powerful methods of healing from PTSD.

4. Learning to meditate and asking help from the Angel of Restoration would help immensely.

CHAPTER 14: DEPRESSION

Summary

Many cases of depression are the direct result of a major emotional upheaval such as loss of a loved one, loss of property, betrayal, etc. there are many physical triggers for depression as well and it is important to check for these factors before you decide on the healing process. The triggers are - adrenal dysfunction, viral infection (EBV), heavy metal and other toxins and electrolyte deficiency.

Each one of these factors has the ability to affect the chemical balance in the brain and cause depression. Since healing needs to counter the underlying factors that cause the health condition, it is important that the correct cause is identified. Just knowing the reason for depression can be a giant step forward towards healing.

There are specific foods that can help defeat depression; they are avocados, kale, apricots, coconut oil, sprouts, walnuts, cilantro, hemp seeds, wild blueberries and spinach. A list of herbal supplements that can restore mind and body health is below.

Healing Herbs & Supplements

Vitamin B12 (as methylcobalamin and/ or adenosylcobalamin): reinforces the central nervous system and brain

Spirulina (from Hawaii): removes heavy metals from the brain and central nervous system

Nascent iodine: supports the thyroid and adrenal glands

44

Melatonin: minimizes brain inflammation and helps grow new neurons

Ester-C: repairs damaged neurotransmitters and strengthens the adrenal glands. Also helps remove toxins from your system

Licorice root: strengthens the thyroid and adrenal glands. Slows the ability of virus cells to reproduce

Ginkgo leaf: supports neurotransmitters

Lemon balm: soothes the central nervous system and limits inflammation

Ashwagandha: Supports the thyroid and adrenal glands

Vitamin D3: strengthens the thyroid and adrenal glands. Also lessens inflammation.

GABA (gamma-Aminobutyric acid): reinforces neuropeptides and neurotransmitters

EPA & DHA (eicosapentaenoic acid and docosahexaenoic acid): fixes and enhances the central nervous system. Purchase plant based not fish based

5-HTP (5-hydroxytryptophan): strengthens neurotransmitters

B-complex: protects the body from the effects of an emotional crisis

Magnesium: soothes muscle tension & relaxes the central nervous system

California poppy: reinforces neurotransmitters and soothes overactive neurons

Kava-kava: lessens stress and calms the central nervous system

Vitamin E: reinforces the central nervous system.

Rhodiola: reinforces the thyroid and adrenal glands; supports the vascular system.

Recap of Chapter 14:

1. The main cause recognized for depression is emotional trauma. Stress trauma is also gaining recognitions in the medical community.

2. Besides the emotional and mental side, there are physical factors that can cause depression and it is important that you know about them - adrenal dysfunction, viral infection (EBV), heavy metal and other toxins and electrolyte deficiency.

3. Healing can be achieved quickest if the factors that cause depression are identified correctly.

CHAPTER 15: PREMENSRTUAL SYNDROME AND MENOPAUSE

Summary

The symptoms relating to premenstrual syndrome and menopause include hot flushes, irritability, fatigue, and heart palpitations. The medical fraternities promptly labeled this as an "It's all in your head disease" that was common to women. The blame was fixed on hormones since women who experienced these symptoms were middle aged.

As soon as the label was given it was found that men too suffer from similar symptoms. However, the pharmaceutical companies riding the wave of a new discovery, maintained that it was a "woman's condition" and soon men felt too embarrassed to talk about it. It is in fact the EBV showing its symptoms.

The first signs of "menopausal" symptoms surfaced early in the 1950s. Before that there was no mention of such a condition. This coincides with the beginning of EBV, which appeared in early 1900. As it went through the stages, it took about five decades to start showing symptoms. Add to that the overexposure to radiation from the shoe-fitting fluoroscope, which poisoned millions of women. The third cause was DDT, which was applied everywhere in the 1940s.

These symptoms are not caused by PMS or menopause, instead these are the result of toxins, EBV and thyroid conditions. While menopausal women are still treated with HRT and BHRT, the treatment does not come out as a success in the majority of cases. The fact that young women, and men, also suffer from the same problems confirms that it is not menopause that causes these symptoms.

The truth is that these symptoms are caused by a mix of various factors such as infection, stress, toxins from the environment and certain deficiencies. It is more pronounced in women who menstruate or are going through menopause because at that time, the body is already stressed out and hence, all other symptoms are easier to observe.

There are many foods that help support the reproductive system; the best are cucumbers, spinach, black grapes, asparagus, apples, black beans, avocados, sesame tahini and wild blueberries. They will help by reducing inflammation, keeping hormone levels balanced and preventing hot flashes. A list of helpful herbs and supplements is given below.

Healing Herbs & Supplements (For General Symptoms)

-Silver hydrosol: kills bacteria and viruses on contact and reinforces the immune system.

-Zinc: supports the immune system and kills viruses

-Licorice root: supports the adrenal glands

-L-lysine: impairs virus cells movement

-Vitamin B12 (as methylcobalamin and/ or adenosylcobalamin): supports the central nervous system

-Nascent iodine: strengthens the endocrine system

-Ashwagandha: balance cortisol production and strengthens the adrenal glands

-Barley grass juice extract powder: helps digestion, cleanses the liver and introduces alkalinity

-Olive leaf: kills fungi, bacteria, and viruses

-Monolaurin: kills bacteria, viruses and non beneficial microbes

-Spirulina (from Hawaii): supports the endocrine system

-Ginseng: strengthens the adrenal glands

<u>Healing Herbs & Supplements</u> (For Reproductive Systems)

-Nettle leaf: lessens inflammation in the reproductive system

-Wild yam: helps stabilize estrogen and progesterone levels

-Schisandra berry: flushes extra estrogen from the body

-Hawthorn berry: supports the ovaries

-Vitex (chaste tree berry): helps regulate the menstrual cycle

-Red clover blossom: removes non beneficial hormones stored in organs

-Sage: fights abnormal cell growth in the cervix

-Folic acid: replenishes the uterus

-B-complex: provides reproductive system with essential vitamins

-Vitamin D3: balances the immune and reproductive systems

-Vitamin E: reinforces the central nervous system and helps blood circulation

-EPA & DHA (eicosapentaenoic acid and docosahexaenoic acid): purchase plant based not fish

Recap of Chapter 15:

1. PMS and Menopause symptoms are not seen only in women; men have it too.

2. The symptoms are caused by one or a cluster of factors which include EBV, heavy metal poisoning, and other toxins.

3. Healing is possible provided you identify the real cause behind the problem. It is important that serious attention is given to all the possible factors that could cause the symptoms.

4. HRT and BHRT is not the answer to the PMS and menopause symptoms, though some may benefit from it.

CHAPTER 16: LYME DISEASE

Summary

The medical fraternity has wrongly identified a bacteria called, "Borrelia burgdorferi" that comes from the bite of a tick that lived on deer. This is not what caused Lyme disease. Later, they named other parasites as the cause for the disease, such as the Bartonella and Babesia. In fact, none of these bacteria have yet been found in a tick.

Lyme disease is caused by a virus. People who carry the EBV, HHV-6, shingles, cytomegalovirus and other viruses develop the symptoms of what the medical fraternity calls Lyme disease. There are many triggers that onset the symptoms of Lyme disease such as, mold, mercury-based dental filling, mercury in any form, pesticides, death of a loved one, emotional trauma, excessive stress (at home or office), sting from bees, bite of spider/ ticks, recreational drugs, antibiotics, drug abuse, insomnia, financial stress, serious physical injury, and so on.

To heal, you need to approach Lyme disease as a viral infection. There are certain foods that can help your body recover from the symptoms of Lyme disease such as onions, apricots, cinnamon, garlic, celery, radishes, wild blueberries, asparagus and star anise. They can kill viral cells and help repair brain cells.

Below is a list of healing herbs and how they help in combating the diseases. They accelerate healing; strengthen the immune system and give time for the body to restore itself.

Healing Herbs & Supplements

- **Silver hydrosol:** kills viruses on contact

-**Lemon balm:** helps reduce the strain on the immune system

-**Zinc:** lessens inflammatory reactions to viral neurotoxins in the herpes family

-**Licorice root:** slows virus cells from being able to reproduce

-**L-lysine:** impairs virus cells from being able to reproduce

-**Lomatium root:** flushes bacterial toxins from the body

-**Reishi mushrooms:** strengthen the immune system by supporting lymphocytes, platelets, and neutrophils

-**Thyme:** kills viruses on contact

-**Astaxanthin:** helps restore virus damaged nerves and brain tissue

-**Nascent iodine:** reinforces and supports the endocrine system

Recap of Chapter 16:

1. Lyme disease is not caused by tick bites or by bacteria.

2. Lyme disease cannot be cured by antibiotics; it rather helps it flare up.

3. This is a viral infection that rears its head in various ways and the only way to fight it is to repress the virus and push it into a dormant state.

4. It is possible to get rid of Lyme disease with the foods and herbs described here.

Part IV

Part IV comes with seven chapters, each showcasing a facet of healing the body, mind and soul. It talks about gut health, which is at the center of the wellbeing of the body, teaches how to get rid of toxins that have settled in the brain and body, advises on the right foods to eat and what to avoid, explains the fallacy of the "fruit fear", gives instruction about how to cleanse your body with the "28 day healing cleanse", teaches how to meditate to relieve stress and lastly, how to call for help from angels.

CHAPTER 17: GUT HEALTH

Summary

Your gut is one of the key foundations to your health which makes it the perfect place to start healing from the inside out. The gut includes the small intestine, the stomach, the gallbladder, the liver and the large intestine. It is responsible for properly expelling toxins from the body and also making sure you absorb the nutrients from the foods you eat. The most common ailments involving the gut include general stomach pain, gastritis, gastric spasms, irritable bowel syndrome, indigestion and poor digestion, leaky gut syndrome, and acid reflux among others.

Ammonia Permeability, when there is too little hydrochloric acid in your stomach, is often mislabeled as leaky gut syndrome or intestinal permeability. This leads to the question, how do I rebuild hydrochloric acid? The answer is very simple, on an empty stomach drink a 16 ounce glass of fresh celery juice. Do not blend it with other fruits as the stomach prefers it alone which allows it to begin its repair work quickly. The process is as follows

1. While on an empty stomach rinse your celery with water

2. Juice the celery by itself as anything else will disrupt its effectiveness

3. Lastly drink the juice immediately

This works because celery contains mineral salts that are bonded with many bioactive trace minerals and nutrients. Over time the mineral salts and nutrients completely restore your stomach's hydrochloric acid. **Rebuilding hydrochloric acid and strengthening your digestive system is the first step to healing any gut related issue.**

Next we'll focus on removing toxic heavy metals which can release poisons directly into your gut. Luckily they are relatively easy to get rid of with the options below.

1. Cilantro: consume half a cup daily in a smoothie or salad

2. Parsley: consume a quarter cup daily in a smoothie or salad

3. Zeolite: this is a mineralized clay, purchase in liquid form

4. Spirulina (from Hawaii): in powdered form mix 1 teaspoon daily into water/smoothie

5. Garlic: consume 2 fresh cloves daily

6. Sage: consume 2 tablespoons daily

7. L-Glutamine: in powdered form mix one teaspoon in water or smoothie

8. Plantain leaf: make tea from this herb and drink daily

9. Red clover blossom: 2 tablespoons will make 2 cups of tea, consume daily

There are a great many fads and myths about the gut but it is important not to get caught up in them. A few examples are hydrochloric acid supplements, sodium bicarbonate, consuming diatomaceous earth, gallbladder blush, fermented foods and apple cider vinegar. The myth that these methods are helpful is unproductive and even reckless in certain situations.

Recap of Chapter 17:

1. A healthy gut means a health body and mind. Almost everything centers upon the health of your gut and it is of paramount importance that you keep it healthy and working optimally.

2. There are many myths about the gut, many of which are supported by the medical community today. It is important that you learn to differentiate between the truth and myth.

3. The foods that you eat decide your health. Foods which have live bacteria are beneficial to the gut. Foods which have been cooked or pasteurized are no longer beneficial.

4. The "hydrochloric acid" in your stomach cannot be recreated artificially because it is actually a mix of seven different acids.

5. Only elevated micro-organisms can naturally restore the balance of good bacteria in the gut.

6. You can remove metal toxins from your gut very effectively with the help of herbs and easy-to-find substances such as cilantro, parsley, zeolite (clay), Spirulina, garlic, L-glutamine, plantain leaf and red clover blossom, among others. Each one of these options can help with detoxification.

CHAPTER 18: FREEING YOUR BRAIN AND BODY OF TOXINS

Summary

Mercury was revered as a miracle cure for all ailments for so long that even after discovering its devastating toxicity it was still not completely eliminated from industrial and medical uses. In fact adulation for mercury didn't slow until the mid 1800s.

Mercury can be passed on through generations through genes and from mother to child. The modern human being still suffers from this poison. A huge list of ailments are caused directly by mercury exposure such as thyroid disorders, hair loss, depression, ADHD, autism, cancer, epilepsy and so much more. Alzheimer's Diseases is one hundred percent caused by mercury.

To regain and maintain your health, both mental and physical, you need to rid your body of the mercury that has accumulated over the years. It is important that you recognize the sources of mercury that could percolate into your body such as seafood, dental amalgams and water with fluoride are some of the primary sources of neurotoxins, both from mercury and aluminum.

For detoxification you should consume the following five items daily, i.e. barley grass juice extract powder, Spirulina (preferably of Hawaii origin), cilantro, wild blueberries (exclusively from Maine) and Atlantic dulse. For optimal results, you would need to consume each one of these items within 24 hours from one another. The use of chlorella is not recommended.

Detoxification is by itself an extremely powerful health tool. It empowers the body to function optimally, and one of the major and most important functions is to heal itself.

Recap of Chapter 18:

1. Mercury is one of the oldest causes for production of neurotoxins in the body. Hailed as a health elixir for more than 2,500 years, it created havoc through generations.

2. It is important to recognize the primary sources of mercury poisoning so you can stay away from it.

3. It is also important to know that most of the serious ailments that plague human beings today have a connection to mercury exposure and poisoning.

4. There are many methods that can remove heavy metals from the body; these methods use various herbs for the purpose.

5. Detoxification of heavy metals from your body would improve the quality of your life and longevity a great deal.

CHAPTER19: WHAT NOT TO EAT

Summary

It is important to avoid foods which poison the body. Often poisons might not affect your health right away, but they build up and join hands with other crating toxins that will make you vulnerable and ill.

All genetically modified organisms (GMO) should be excluded from your diet. This category would include corn, soy, canola oil, processed beet sugar, eggs, dairy products, pork, farmed fish, gluten, MSG (food additive), all natural flavoring, artificial flavors and sweeteners and citric acid.

Health supplements are dangerous as well. Among those which need to be avoided are L-carnitine, glandular supplements, whey protein, fish oil supplements and iron supplements among others.

Try to draw the benefits of these supplements from natural foods. You need to focus on your diet and consciously eliminate all foods that you know are harmful and even those that you suspect do you harm.

Recap of Chapter 19:

1. All genetically modified organisms need to be eliminated from your diet.

2. Beware that health supplements can be as harmful and poisonous as GMOs.

3. It is always best to choose to draw vitamins, minerals and other nutrients directly from food rather than health supplements.

CHAPTER 20: FRUIT FEAR

Summary

There are those that think fruit is a wrong food because it contains high amounts of sugar. Nothing could be further from the truth. Just as all types of water are not the same, so all types of sugar are not the same. You would not compare rain water with drinking water, or distilled water to aquarium water. Similarly, contrary to what the current belief is about fruits, their consumption on a regular basis is highly recommended.

The sugar you have to fear does not come from the fruit but from refined foods. Unfortunately, people tend to confuse a pound of fruit with one of sugar. It is not the right way to calculate the sugar content. A pound of refined sugar equals a pound of sugar; a pound of fruit comes with life-saving fiber, phytonutrients, pectin, antioxidants, vitamins and so much more.

Fruits are a vital part of a healthy diet. It is refined sugar that you should avoid at all costs. Another major fallacy that has become the trend today is to eat fruits as per their season and avoid them if they are available outside the season. Fruits, as long as they are organically grown, are beneficial anytime of the year.

Another myth that needs to be debunked is that fruits that are ripened after they have been plucked are better than those which were plucked already ripened in the tree. This is not true. Plants too need to follow a certain cycle to be edible and full of benefits. When cut too early or removed too early, many of the beneficial processes that are normally triggered while the fruit matures in the tree, no longer take place. A fad that claims to produce too much too quick is the plantation of hybrid fruit trees. These trees grow quickly, flower quickly and bear fruit quickly as well. While the fruits look appetizing and handsome, they should rather be avoided for they are more harmful than helpful.

Fruit is your best friend. It can reverse and delay aging, boost the immune system, stamina, brain function, keep infections at bay and ensure the best nutrition for your body. Fruits of any type and any season should be eaten. Fruits are well known as the natural killers of viruses and a good number of bacteria. Some very serious ailments – ALS, Alzheimer's, Parkinson's, dementia, memory loss, etc. could be prevented by regular consumption of fruit.

Recap of Chapter 20:

1. Fruits are must-have additions to your daily diet.

2. Regular consumption of fruits will eliminate and prevent many ailments, including cancer and virus attacks.

3. Fruits are vital for your gut's health and therefore, your overall health.

4. Fruits are excellent in slowing down and even reversing aging symptoms.

5. Alzheimer's, dementia, and many neurological diseases such as Parkinson's and ALS can be prevented by regular consumption of fruit.

6. Fruits promote longevity, brain function, heart health and many other aspects of health.

CHAPTER 21: THE 28-DAY HEALING CLEANSE

Summary

Just like an abused vehicle is bound to collapse one day unless the oil, valves & bushes are changed, the human body too can become overwhelmed and give in to illness. It is important to cleanse your body of the toxins that build up over time.

The human body is designed to repair itself; but to do that it needs to have a diet free from toxins or be given enough time to eliminate these on its own. When none of the options happen, expect trouble. To ensure optimal functioning of your body, you need to perform cleansings regularly. This will eliminate the toxins that get assimilated in the body through pollution, wrong diet, stress, and other factors discussed in this book.

The author advises that you go for a 28-day cleanse plan, which contains exclusively raw vegetables and fruits. This method not only provides your body with the maximum intake of healthy nutrients, but also helps elimination of toxins. It helps both body and soul in the most extreme positive manner. This plan is designed to detoxify, alkalize, remineralize your body and mend your soul.

It is best that during the cleansing process you would choose to take rest – and avoid any type of stress. As the body eliminates toxins you would feel a wide variety of symptoms – some not so pleasant. Meditating and praying during this period is recommended for mental detoxification.

Recap of Chapter 21:

1. Cleansing is a very important function that is required at regular intervals.

2. The 28-day cleansing plan is a method that uses only raw vegetables and fruits to detoxify your body and mind and ensure optimal functioning of all the systems.

3. It is important that you take rest from work when you are going through the cleansing period as toxin elimination can make you feel sick at some point of time.

4. In case you cannot do the 28-day cleansing program, you could do as much as you can and work towards achieving the 28-day plan.

5. Meditation is an important component during this period as this frees the mind from negative thought and fills it with good thoughts.

CHAPTER 22: SOUL HEALING MEDITATION AND TECHNIQUES

Summary

Unhappiness often invites illnesses and therefore, it is important to learn how to heal the soul and revive the spirit to feel whole and rejuvenated.

The emotional detox will help you release negative feelings that keep you from following your destiny in life, keep you from being happy, healthy and grateful for your life. This can be achieved through meditation.

There are many types of meditation that will heal your mind, your heart and you soul and bring you closer to the Universe, the Divine Power or God. Such methods include watching waves on the beach, meditating in the midst of trees, meditating while watching birds flying, bee watching meditation, collecting stones, sun bathing, picking fruit, watching your garden grow and any other thing that you feel could help your mind soar high and free. You are encouraged to be creative and adventurous in finding your own methods.

Sunsets can be especially healing for the soul and mind. Sunset watching is recommended for those who feel heartbroken, betrayed or let down by loved ones. Sunsets and sunrises have the power to prove that life has much more to give and helps inner healing.

It's important to accept that you are working with the highest power there is in the Universe. By doing so you will realize and internalize that there is much more to life than the daily trials life throws at you. This is a method to make you conscious of the larger picture and hence, gain the ability to shift your perspective and enrich your life through positive affirmation, thoughts and actions.

Recap of Chapter 22:

1. There is an important connect between health of the soul, mind and body. A healthy mind would ensure a healthy soul and body.

2. It is important to cleanse your mind and soul of negative emotions just as it is important to clean your body of toxins.

3. The way to do that is through meditation. Meditation is of many kinds and can be anything that sets your mind free and helps you heal from inside out.

4. You can be as creative as you want with your style of meditation. It is not necessary to follow any type of set rules; the only requirement is to eliminate negative feelings and thoughts and replace them with positive ones.

5. It is important to learn to look at the larger picture, to change your perspective about life so as to not allow day-to-day problems affect your soul, mind, feelings, or thoughts.

6. A connect with the Higher Power – God, Universe, Divinity, Cosmos – is important to the cleansing of the soul and promoting best health.

CHAPTER 23: ESSENTIAL ANGELS

Summary

In this chapter we will describe emotional scenarios in the following terms- "drought", "flood", "heat wave" and "earthquake". "Drought" is when things dry up and don't go your way; "flood' is when you get too much of everything and you feel overwhelmed by it all; "heat wave" is when your life is filled with stress caused by work, responsibilities and various issues; and lastly, "earthquake" is when you face some devastating effect in your life like a death, an accident or something similar.

At any time you want, you can call out for help to angels and they are always happy to help. To get them to listen to your call and help you, you need to know two things – (i) how to call them and (ii) whom to call.

There are two categories of angels – those who have a name and those who are unnamed or unknown. Each category has its benefits and you are free to call one or a group of angels to help you. There are 21 essential angels each with their own powers so you should choose which one, or which ones, you need to help you overcome your problems. When talking about those without names, one of the greatest plus points of invoking these category of angels is that they are most eager to help. There are 144,000 unknown angels - and all are ready and eager to come to your aid.

There is a special way to invoke help from angels, i.e. you have to ask it aloud and not in mind. You need to be sincere, honest and articulate in what you are asking; and the prayer or call to the angel for help should be spoken. You can whisper it if you want, but it has to come in words formed by your mouth – clear, concise and with faith. Having said that, the author explains that not all the prayers may be answered, but that does not mean that angels do not want to come to your aid. It often means that what you ask may not be in your best interests, and/ or God/ Universe has other plans for you, better plans for you.

Recap of Chapter 23:

1. Angels are always ready to help you when you are in need.

2. There are 21 essential angels who are named and have definite powers, and 144,000 unknown angels who have no name and are most eager to come and help you manage the problems you may encounter in your life.

3. To get angels come to your aid, you need to ask their help with spoken words. It has to be a proper request that names clearly what you want them to do for you.

4. Not all prayers may be answered; but when this happens it is always because there is something better waiting for you.

Important Facts Recap

RECAP- CHAPTER 1: ORIGINS OF THE MEDICAL MEDIUM

1. The author gains his special powers from "The Spirit of the Most High", a being who claims to be next to only God.

2. The Spirit, constantly talks to the author telling him clearly and accurately what the diagnosis is, what causes it and how it can be cured.

3. The Spirit also helped the author repair cars.

4. Anthony Williams commits to his gift and agrees to be the Medical Medium as Spirit wants in return for the life of his dog, Augustine whom the Spirit saves.

RECAP - CHAPTER 2: THE TRUTH ABOUT MYSTERY ILLNESSES

1. Millions of people worldwide suffer from mystery diseases.

2. There are three types of mystery illnesses, i.e. diseases that have no name (yet), diseases which have no effective treatment, and diseases that are misdiagnosed.

3. It is NOT true that the body attacks itself. All diseases that fall under the category of autoimmune diseases are mystery illnesses.

4. It is NOT in your head; the symptoms you feel are true, even when doctors have no valid answers.

5. Spirit has all the answers and he wants the world to benefit from this knowledge through Anthony Williams.

6. You can be cured of whatever diseases you are suffering from.

RECAP- CHAPTER 3: EPSTEIN BARR VIRUS, CHRONIC FATIGUE SYNDROME AND FIBROMYALGIA

1. Discovered in 1964, the EBV has been around since the 1900's and has mutated a lot since then.

2. The medical fraternity knows about only ONE strain of the EBV; there are more than 60 varieties, which are not yet discovered.

3. More than 225 million people in the USA alone suffer from some type of EBV.

4. The 60 varieties are grouped into 6 groups with roughly 10 types per group.

5. The ultimate goal of the EBV is to reach and inflame your central nervous system.

6. There are 4 stages of the EBV infection; it takes sometimes decades for the virus to move from one stage to another.

7. EBV is easily curable; the difficult part is to find it.

RECAP- CHAPTER 4: MULTIPLE SCLEROSIS

1. Multiple sclerosis is often EBV misdiagnosed.

2. MS (misdiagnosed or real) is completely curable; with the right foods and supplements, you can be free from it in 3-18 months depending upon your condition.

3. To confirm that your MS is actually EBV, you may look for signs of cofactors in the body such as streptococcus, H.pylori, Candida, Cytomegalovirus and presence of heavy metals (mercury, copper and aluminum).

RECAP- CHAPTER 5: RHEUMATOID ARTHRITIS

1. Rheumatoid Arthritis is not an autoimmune disease since the body never attacks itself.

2. RA is completely curable, though the medical fraternity declared it as incurable.

3. The methods used today for diagnosing RA are not adequate.

4. RA is a form EBV and can be completely eliminated within 2-24 months

RECAP- CHAPTER 6: HYPOTHYROIDISM AND HASHIMOTO'S THYROIDITIS

1. Hypothyroidism and Hashimoto's disease both are caused by the EBV.
2. Tests known today are not adequate for diagnosing thyroid problems.
3. Thyroid conditions caused by EBV are completely and easily curable.

RECAP- CHAPTER 7: TYPE 2 DIABETES AND HYPOGLYCEMIA

1. Type 2 diabetes and hypoglycemia are not caused by sugar abuse. The problem starts with malfunctioning adrenal glands.
2. Besides a long list of healing foods, you should include fruits in your diet; it is the high-protein diet that causes you most harm while the fruits heal.
3. Caught in time, both the pancreas and liver will regenerate as all damage is reversible.
4. Type 2 diabetes and hypoglycemia are totally curable.

RECAP- CHAPTER 8: ADRENAL FATIGUE

1. Adrenal fatigue is similar to mental breakdown (of the glands) and results in erratic production of adrenaline; it could be either too much or too less.

2. It is very important to address the mental and emotional condition while attempting to heal. Strong emotions (negative) are as bad as stress for the adrenal glands.

3. Complete healing is possible with natural foods and substances.

4. Meditation is recommended to enhance the ability of body and mind to handle stress and emotional upheavals.

5. In many instances, the underlying cause is an infection of the EBV, yet unknown to the medical fraternity.

RECAP- CHAPTER 9: CANDIDA

1. Everybody has Candida in their gut; it is a friendly and useful fungus, which lives in the gut and helps digestion.

2. When Candida comes positive in tests, it is always an indication of an underlying problem; this is a cofactor to many infections.

3. It is possible to get rid of Candida, but to do so you need eat plenty of fruits and maintain a low fat, low protein diet.

4. No antibiotics or anti-fungal medication should be taken for Candida as this would produce the opposite effect.

RECAP- CHAPTER 10: MIGRAINES

1. Migraines are often caused by a cluster of 2-3 factors; it is important to identify all triggers.

2. There are certain foods that aggravate/ trigger migraines; they need to be eliminated from the diet.

3. There are many other triggers - previously known by the medical fraternity – that cause migraines; careful investigation is required to identify the exact triggers.

4. It is possible to be completely cured of migraines with the right foods and supplements.

RECAP- CHAPTER 11: SHINGLES – TRUE CAUSE OF COLITIS, TMJ, DIABETIC NEUROPATHY AND MORE

1. Shingles are often the underlying cause for many of the mystery illnesses of today, such as MS, colitis, Bell's palsy, Lyme disease and so on.

2. It is important that you avoid all medication that lowers the efficiency of your immune system.

3. It is possible to eliminate shingles from your system completely and permanently – with the food and supplements recommended in the book.

RECAP- CHAPTER 12: ATTENTION DEFICIT/ HYPERACTIVITY DISORDER AND AUTISM

1. The causes behind ADHD and autism are not well defined by the medical fraternity.

2. The ailments are the result of deposit of heavy metals in the canal that separates the right from the left brain hemispheres.

3. Healing foods diet and detoxification is the path to healing for ADHD and autistic children.

RECAP- CHAPTER 13: POST TRAUMATIC STRESS DISORDER

1. There are two types of PTSD - the first type is that which the medical fraternity knows and treats and results from a major setback in the patient's life; the second type is the non-recognized PTSD or that the patient does not dwell on.

2. The main reason for the symptoms of PTSD is depletion of glucose – and not electrolytes as it is believed today.

3. Creating positive experiences as new reference points is one of the most powerful methods of healing from PTSD.

4. Learning to meditate and asking help from Angel of Restoration would help immensely besides switching the healing food and supplements.

RECAP- CHAPTER 14: DEPRESSION

1. The main cause recognized for depression is emotional trauma. Stress trauma is also gaining recognitions in the medical community.

2. Besides the emotional and mental side, there are physical factors that can cause depression and it is important that you know about them - adrenal dysfunction, viral infection (EBV), heavy metal and other toxins and electrolyte deficiency.

3. Healing can be achieved quickest if the factors that cause depression are identified correctly.

RECAP- CHAPTER 15: PREMENSTRUAL SYNDROME AND MENOPAUSE

1. PMS and Menopause symptoms are not seen only in women; men have it too.

2. The symptoms are caused by one or a cluster of factors which include EBV, heavy metal poisoning, and other toxins.

3. Healing is possible provided you identify the real cause behind the problem. It is important that serious attention is given to all the possible factors that could cause the symptoms.

4. HRT and BHRT is not the answer to PMS and menopause symptoms, though some may be benefitted from it.

RECAP- CHAPTER 16: LYME DISEASE

1. Lyme disease is not caused by tick bites or by bacteria.

2. Lyme disease cannot be cured by antibiotics; it rather helps it flare up.

3. This is a viral infection that rears its head in various ways and the only way to fight it is to repress the virus and push it into a dormant state.

4. It is possible to get rid of Lyme disease – with the method outlined in this chapter and the foods and herbs descried.

RECAP- CHAPTER 17: GUT HEALTH

1. A healthy gut means a health body and mind. Almost everything centers upon the health of your gut and it is of paramount importance that you keep it healthy and working optimally.

2. There are many myths about the gut, many of which are supported by the medical community today. It is important that you learn to differentiate between the truth and myth.

3. The foods that you eat decide your health. Foods which have live bacteria are beneficial to the gut. Foods which have been cooked or pasteurized are no longer beneficial.

4. The "hydrochloric acid" in your stomach cannot be recreated artificially because it is actually a mix of seven different acids.

5. Only elevated micro-organisms can naturally restore the balance of good bacteria in the gut.

6. You can remove metal toxins from your gut very effectively with the help of herbs and easy-to-find substances such as cilantro, parsley, zeolite (clay), Spirulina, garlic, L-glutamine, plantain leaf and red clover blossom, among others. Each one of these options can help with detoxification.

RECAP- CHAPTER 18: FREEING YOUR BRAIN AND BODY OF TOXINS

1. Mercury is one of the oldest causes for production of neurotoxins in the body. Hailed as a health elixir for more than 2,500 years, it has created havoc through generations.

2. It is important to recognize the primary sources of mercury poisoning so you can stay away from it.

3. It is also important to know that most of the serious ailments that plague human beings today have a connection to mercury exposure and poisoning.

4. There are many methods that can remove heavy metals from the body; these methods use various herbs for the purpose.

5. Detoxification of heavy metals from your body would improve the quality of your life and longevity a great deal.

RECAP- CHAPTER 19: WHAT NOT TO EAT

1. All genetically modified organisms need to be eliminated from your diet.

2. Beware that health supplements can be as harmful and poisonous as GMOs.

3. It is always best to choose to draw vitamins, minerals and other nutrients directly from food rather than health supplements.

RECAP- CHAPTER 20: FRUIT FEAR

1. Fruits are must-have additions to your daily diet.

2. Regular consumption of fruits will eliminate and prevent many ailments, including cancer and virus attacks.

3. Fruits are vital for your gut's health and therefore, your overall health.

4. Fruits are excellent in slowing down and even reversing aging symptoms.

5. Alzheimer's, dementia, and many neurological diseases such as Parkinson's and ALS can be prevented by regular consumption of fruit.

6. Fruits promote longevity, brain function, heart health and many other aspects of health.

RECAP- CHAPTER 21: THE 28-DAY HEALING CLEANSE

1. Cleansing is a very important function that is required at regular intervals.

2. The 28-day cleansing plan is a method that uses only raw vegetables and fruits to detoxify your body and mind and ensure optimal functioning of all the systems.

3. It is important that you take rest from work when you are going through the cleansing period as toxin elimination can make you feel sick at some point of time.

4. In case you cannot do the 28-day cleansing program, you could do as much as you can and work towards achieving the 28-day plan.

5. Meditation is an important component during this period as this frees the mind from negative thought and fills it with good thoughts.

RECAP- CHAPTER 22: SOUL-HEALING MEDITATIONS AND TECHNIQUES

1. There is an important connect between health of the soul, mind and body. A healthy mind would ensure a healthy soul and body.

2. It is important to cleanse your mind and soul of negative emotions just as it is important to clean your body of toxins.

3. The way to do that is through meditation. Meditation is of many kinds and can be anything that sets your mind free and helps you heal from inside out.

4. You can be as creative as you want with your style of meditation. It is not necessary to follow any type of set rules; the only requirement is to eliminate negative feelings and thoughts and replace them with positive ones.

5. It is important to learn to look at the larger picture, to change your perspective about life so as to not

allow day-to-day problems affect your soul, mind, feelings, or thoughts.

6. A connection with the Higher Power – God, Universe, Divinity and Cosmos – is important to the cleansing of the soul and promoting best health.

RECAP- CHAPTER 23: ESSENTIAL ANGELS

1. Angels are always ready to help you when you are in need.

2. There are 21 essential angels who are named and have definite powers, and 144,000 unknown angels who have no name and are most eager to come and help you manage the problems you may encounter in your life.

3. To get angels to come to your aid, you need to ask for their help with spoken words. It has to be a proper request that names clearly what you want them to do for you.

4. Not all prayers may be answered; but when this happens it is always because there is something better waiting for you.

Commentary & Discussion Questions

OUR ANALYSIS

This book was written with an intention to shatter the myths about today's illnesses, their causes, methods of healing and prevention. The author introduces himself as a lay person who is guided by a live and very powerful being who calls himself "The Spirit of the Most High" or "Spirit" as the author chooses to address him.

Spirit, who claims to be second to only God in powers, says that he represents the word, "compassion". He tells Anthony William – the author of the book – that he would help people to heal, body, mind and soul. Spirit starts teaching Anthony to scan bodies for disease and identify illnesses and their cures.

Anthony goes on to explain that Spirit reveals a few critical secrets that would help human kind understand what causes mystery illnesses and how to cure them. The book makes two major statements that are meant to change the way medical science looks at mystery illnesses. The first is that the human body never attacks itself, under no circumstances; and the second is that the so-called mystery illnesses which are listed under unexplained mystery "autoimmune diseases" are actually caused by the Epstein - Barr virus or EBV.

Each chapter is dedicated to explain the role of the virus – there are 60 strains of it – and its life cycle. The virus stays undetected baffling doctors about various symptoms because it is adept at hiding in the organs of the body while crossing its 4 evolutionary stages. Anthony explains that the EBV's primary aim is to reach the central nervous system.

When the body reacts by targeting any part of the body – causing misdiagnosis of autoimmune diseases – it actually is pointing at the enemy hidden deep inside the body invisible to tests and unknown to the present day medical science.

The book goes ahead and debunks some critical myths that have harmed more than helped human kind. One most important is that all sugar is the same and hence, fruits should be avoided to help healing. Spirit points out through Anthony that fruit sugar is actually the best thing that can happen to the human body. Refined and processed sugars are indeed harmful, but fruit sugars are always beneficial.

It also goes on to disclose that the high-protein, low carbs and no sugar "healthy" diet is a major mistake. The high-protein foods are actually high-fat foods, which trigger serious health problems because it strains the liver, pancreas, the immune system and the adrenal glands.

Another myth is that you can ignore harmful foods if taken in small measures. In the chapter "what not to eat" the author clearly states that all poison, no matter how small the dose, has the capacity to harm the body as toxins build up over years, sometimes over generations.

While explaining the causes of diseases, the author reveals another secret. Mercury poisoning is the root cause of a number of diseases such as ADHD, autism, migraines among others. He also states that Alzheimer is 100 percent caused by mercury poisoning.

The author describes holistic healing methods that involve restoring the health of the gut, eating right, meditation and spiritual connect. It also stresses the fact that the majority of illnesses would actually disappear if the diet is based on (organic) raw vegetables and fruits.

Throughout the book there are case studies that add a new dimension to the information shared in the book. The real-life scenarios described in the case studies connect with the reader on an emotional level and make the book a fascinating read.

Discussion Questions to Get You Thinking

1. What is the greatest secret revealed in the book? Name two others.

2. How does the author prove that the concept of autoimmune diseases is a complete fallacy?

3. Why is it important to focus on the health of the gut to ensure overall body and mind health?

4. How does the EBV manage to stay hidden while causing so many illnesses?

5. What are the most harmful myths of the modern age? What is "fruit fear"?

6. Why it is important to cleanse toxins from the body on a regular basis?

7. Why is the 28-day cleansing plan one of the most powerful health restoration methods?

8. Why does meditation need to be an integral part of the healing process?

9. What types of meditation are best for healing?

10. What are angels and why should you call them for help?

About High Speed Reads

Here at High Speed Reads our goal is to save you time by providing the best summaries possible. We stand out from our competitors by not only including all of the pertinent facts from the subject book but also a personal analysis of the book, easy to follow summaries of each chapter including a list of chapter highlights, a 30 second summary of the entire book and even discussion questions to get you thinking.

As you can see we go above and beyond to make your purchase a pleasant one. If you learned something beneficial from this book please leave a positive review so others can benefit as well. Lastly if you haven't yet make sure you purchase the subject book.

32867179R00057

Made in the USA
San Bernardino, CA
17 April 2016